Francis Frith's

North Somerset

Shepton Mallet, Town Street 1899 44543

Photographic Memories

Francis Frith's
North Somerset

Dennis and Jan Kelsall

First published in the United Kingdom in 2001 by
Frith Book Company Ltd

Hardback Edition 2001
ISBN 1-85937-302-x

British Library Cataloguing in Publication Data

Francis Frith's North Somerset
Dennis and Jan Kelsall

Frith Book Company Ltd
Frith's Barn, Teffont,
Salisbury, Wiltshire SP3 5QP
Tel: +44 (0) 1722 716 376
Email: info@francisfrith.co.uk
www.francisfrith.co.uk

Printed and bound in Great Britain

Front Cover: Cheddar, Entrance to Pass 1908 60134

AS WITH ANY HISTORICAL DATABASE THE FRITH ARCHIVE IS CONSTANTLY BEING CORRECTED AND IMPROVED AND THE PUBLISHERS WOULD WELCOME INFORMATION ON OMISSIONS OR INACCURACIES

Contents

Francis Frith: *Victorian Pioneer*

Francis Frith, Victorian founder of the world-famous photographic archive, was a complex and multi-talented man. A devout Quaker and a highly successful Victorian businessman, he was both philosophic by nature and pioneering in outlook.

By 1855 Francis Frith had already established a wholesale grocery business in Liverpool, and sold it for the astonishing sum of £200,000, which is the equivalent today of over £15,000,000. Now a multi-millionaire, he was able to indulge his passion for travel. As a child he had pored over travel books written by early explorers, and his fancy and imagination had been stirred by family holidays to the sublime mountain regions of Wales and Scotland. 'What a land of spirit-stirring and enriching scenes and places!' he had written. He was to return to these scenes of grandeur in later years to 'recapture the thousands of vivid and tender memories', but with a different purpose. Now in his thirties, and captivated by the new science of photography, Frith set out on a series of pioneering journeys to the Nile regions that occupied him from 1856 until 1860.

Intrigue and Adventure

He took with him on his travels a specially-designed wicker carriage that acted as both dark-room and sleeping chamber. These far-flung journeys were packed with intrigue and adventure. In his life story, written when he was sixty-three, Frith tells of being held captive by bandits, and of fighting 'an awful midnight battle to the very point of surrender with a deadly pack of hungry, wild dogs'. Sporting flowing Arab costume, Frith arrived at Akaba by camel seventy years before Lawrence, where he encountered 'desert princes and rival sheikhs, blazing with jewel-hilted swords'.

During these extraordinary adventures he was assiduously exploring the desert regions bordering the Nile and patiently recording the antiquities and peoples with his camera. He was the first photographer to venture beyond the sixth cataract. Africa was still the mysterious 'Dark Continent', and Stanley and Livingstone's historic meeting was a decade into the future. The conditions for picture taking confound belief. He laboured for hours in his wicker dark-room in the sweltering heat of the desert, while the volatile chemicals fizzed dangerously in their trays. Often he was forced to work in remote tombs and caves where conditions were cooler. Back in London he exhibited his photographs and was 'rapturously cheered' by members of the Royal Society. His reputation as a photographer was made overnight. An eminent modern historian has likened their impact on the population of the time to that on our own generation of the first photographs taken on the surface of the moon.

Venture of a Life-Time

Characteristically, Frith quickly spotted the opportunity to create a new business as a specialist publisher of photographs. He lived in an era of immense and sometimes violent change. For the poor in the early part of Victoria's reign work was a drudge and the hours long, and people had precious little free time to enjoy themselves. Most had no transport other than a cart or gig at their disposal, and had not travelled far beyond the boundaries of their own town or village. However, by the 1870s, the railways had threaded their way across the country, and Bank Holidays and half-day Saturdays had been made obligatory by Act of Parliament. All of a sudden the ordinary working man and his family were able to enjoy days out and see a little more of the world.

With characteristic business acumen, Francis Frith foresaw that these new tourists would enjoy having souvenirs to commemorate their days out. In 1860 he married Mary Ann Rosling and set out with the intention of photographing every city, town and village in Britain. For the next thirty years he travelled the country by train and by pony and trap, producing fine photographs of seaside resorts and beauty spots that were keenly bought by millions of Victorians. These prints were painstakingly pasted into family albums and pored over during the dark nights of winter, rekindling precious memories of summer excursions.

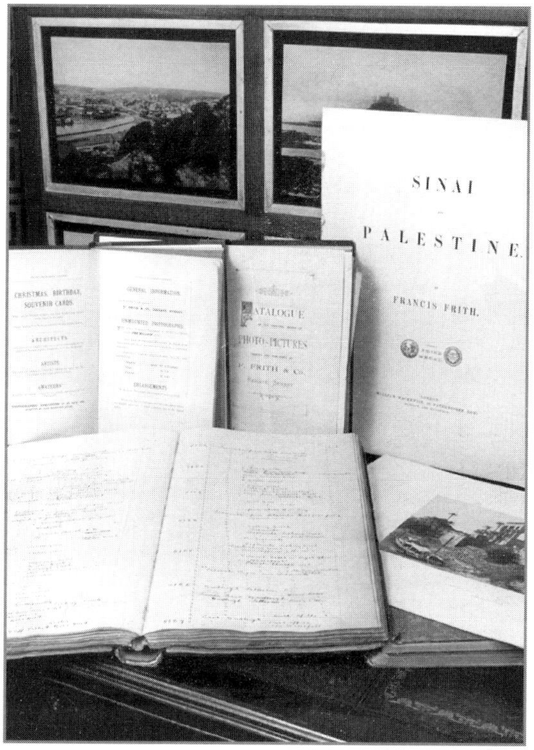

The Rise of Frith & Co

Frith's studio was soon supplying retail shops all over the country. To meet the demand he gathered about him a small team of photographers, and published the work of independent artist-photographers of the calibre of Roger Fenton and Francis Bedford. In order to gain some understanding of the scale of Frith's business one only has to look at the catalogue issued by Frith & Co in 1886: it runs to some 670 pages, listing not only many thousands of views of the British Isles but also many photographs of most European countries, and China, Japan, the USA and Canada – note the sample page shown above from the hand-written *Frith & Co* ledgers detailing pictures taken. By 1890 Frith had created the greatest specialist photographic publishing company in the world,

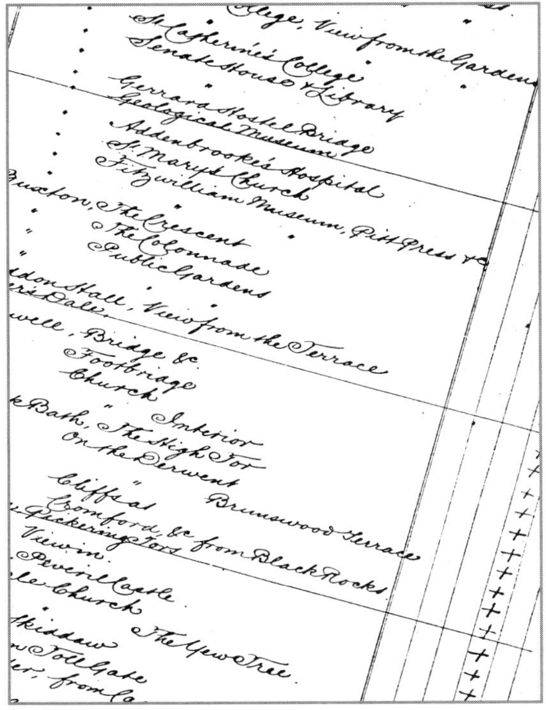

...llege, View from the Gardens
St Catherine's College
Senate House & Library
Gerrard Hostel Bridge
Geological Museum
Addenbrooke's Hospital
St Mary's Church
Fitzwilliam Museum, Pitt Press &c
...uxton, The Crescent
" The Colonnade
" Public Gardens
...don Hall, View from the Terrace
...'s Dale
...well, Bridge &c
Footbridge
Church
...k Bath, The High Tor " Interior
On the Derwent
Cliffs at " Brunswood Terrace
Cromford, &c from Black Rocks
...Pickering Tors
View in
Peveril Castle
...le Church
...kiddaw The Yew Tree
...n Toll Gate
...er, from Ca...

with over 2,000 outlets – more than the combined number that Boots and WH Smith have today! The picture on the right shows the *Frith & Co* display board at Ingleton in the Yorkshire Dales. Beautifully constructed with mahogany frame and gilt inserts, it could display up to a dozen local scenes.

Postcard Bonanza

The ever-popular holiday postcard we know today took many years to develop. In 1870 the Post Office issued the first plain cards, with a pre-printed stamp on one face. In 1894 they allowed other publishers' cards to be sent through the mail with an attached adhesive halfpenny stamp. Demand grew rapidly, and in 1895 a new size of postcard was permitted called the court card, but there was little room for illustration. In 1899, a year after Frith's death, a new card measuring 5.5 x 3.5 inches became the standard format, but it was not until 1902 that the divided back came into being, with address and message on one face and a full-size illustration on the other. *Frith & Co* were in the vanguard of postcard development, and Frith's sons Eustace and Cyril continued their father's monumental task, expanding the number of views offered to the public and recording more and more places in Britain, as the coasts and countryside were opened up to mass travel.

Francis Frith died in 1898 at his villa in Cannes, his great project still growing. The archive he created continued in business for another seventy years. By 1970 it contained over a third of a million pictures of 7,000 cities, towns and villages. The massive photographic record Frith has left to us stands as a living monument to a special and very remarkable man.

Frith's Archive: *A Unique Legacy*

Francis Frith's legacy to us today is of immense significance and value, for the magnificent archive of evocative photographs he created provides a unique record of change in 7,000 cities, towns and villages throughout Britain over a century and more. Frith and his fellow studio photographers revisited locations many times down the years to update their views, compiling for us an enthralling and colourful pageant of British life and character.

We tend to think of Frith's sepia views of Britain as nostalgic, for most of us use them to conjure up memories of places in our own lives with which we have family associations. It often makes us forget that to Francis Frith they were records of daily life as it was actually being lived in the cities, towns and villages of his day. The Victorian age was one of great and often bewildering change for ordinary people, and though the pictures evoke an impression of slower times, life was as busy and hectic as it is today.

We are fortunate that Frith was a photographer of the people, dedicated to recording the minutiae of everyday life. For it is this sheer wealth of visual data, the painstaking chronicle of changes in dress, transport, street layouts, buildings, housing, engineering and landscape that captivates us so much today. His remarkable images offer us a powerful link with the past and with the lives of our ancestors.

See Frith at www.francisfrith.co.uk

Today's Technology

Computers have now made it possible for Frith's many thousands of images to be accessed almost instantly. In the Frith archive today, each photograph is carefully 'digitised' then stored on a CD Rom. Frith archivists can locate a single photograph amongst thousands within seconds. Views can be catalogued and sorted under a variety of categories of place and content to the immediate benefit of researchers.

Inexpensive reference prints can be created for them at the touch of a mouse button, and a wide range of books and other printed materials assembled and published for a wider, more general readership - in the next twelve months over a hundred Frith local history titles will be published! The day-to-day workings of the archive are very different from how they were in Francis Frith's time: imagine the herculean task of sorting through eleven tons of glass negatives as Frith had to do to locate a particular sequence of pictures! Yet the archive still prides itself on maintaining the same high standards of excellence laid down by Francis Frith, including the painstaking cataloguing and indexing of every view.

It is curious to reflect on how the internet now allows researchers in America and elsewhere greater instant access to the archive than Frith himself ever enjoyed. Many thousands of individual views can be called up on screen within seconds on one of the Frith internet sites, enabling people living continents away to revisit the streets of their ancestral home town, or view places in Britain where they have enjoyed holidays. Many overseas researchers welcome the chance to view special theme selections, such as transport, sports, costume and ancient monuments.

We are certain that Francis Frith would have heartily approved of these modern developments in imaging techniques, for he himself was always working at the very limits of Victorian photographic technology.

The Value of the Archive Today

Because of the benefits brought by the computer, Frith's images are increasingly studied by social historians, by researchers into genealogy and ancestory, by architects, town planners, and by teachers and schoolchildren involved in local history projects.

In addition, the archive offers every one of us an opportunity to examine the places where we and our families have lived and worked down the years. Highly successful in Frith's own era, the archive is now, a century and more on, entering a new phase of popularity.

The Past in Tune with the Future

Historians consider the Francis Frith Collection to be of prime national importance. It is the only archive of its kind remaining in private ownership and has been valued at a million pounds. However, this figure is now rapidly increasing as digital technology enables more and more people around the world to enjoy its benefits.

Francis Frith's archive is now housed in an historic timber barn in the beautiful village of Teffont in Wiltshire. Its founder would not recognize the archive office as it is today. In place of the many thousands of dusty boxes containing glass plate negatives and an all-pervading odour of photographic chemicals, there are now ranks of computer screens. He would be amazed to watch his images travelling round the world at unimaginable speeds through network and internet lines.

The archive's future is both bright and exciting. Francis Frith, with his unshakeable belief in making photographs available to the greatest number of people, would undoubtedly approve of what is being done today with his lifetime's work. His photographs, depicting our shared past, are now bringing pleasure and enlightenment to millions around the world a century and more after his death.

North Somerset - *An Introduction*

WITH A LANDSCAPE as rich and varied as any in England, one can imagine that a high degree of pleasurable anticipation pulsed through Francis Frith's veins, when he first arrived in Somerset. With his bulky camera and tripod, glass plates and bottles of chemicals, he toured the county, capturing not only its scenes, but also something of its mood as both a century and an age drew to a close.

Sandwiched between the main body of England and the extremities of Devon and Cornwall, the county is a transition from the soft, mellow limestone hills that are such a feature of the heart of England, to the wild, lonely moorland and rugged coasts that characterise the far west peninsula. The transformation is neither harsh nor sudden, but a spectrum of varying complexions which merge, one into the other, to create one of the country's most attractive landscapes. Although not the largest of counties, it boasts a National Park in Exmoor and three designated Areas of Outstanding Natural Beauty: the Mendip, Quantock and Blackdown hills. Each has its own special quality, expressed in the differing stones of their composition, which have been used to fashion the towns and villages that lie around them. Mention too must be made of Somerset's other great distinctive feature, the Levels. These vast tracts of land are barely above the level of the sea, but penetrate deep into the landmass, where their two-dimensional impressiveness is accentuated by island-like hills, many of which were, in fact, lapped by the tide not that long ago. It is a land rich in legend and history, often with no clear delimiter between the two, whose tendrils reach back into the distant mists of time. But its story is more than mere words, for the landscape is littered with relics and curiosities. Some fired the imagination, others are evidence of events and deeds, all of which are clues to understanding Somerset's past.

The limestone caves at Cheddar have yielded bones of our Palaeolithic ancestors, some of the oldest to be found in the country, and which modern technology has shown to be related to a family living in the nearby village. Elsewhere standing stones and burials are enigmatic symbols of a later age, and hilltops such as Brent Knoll and Glastonbury Tor bear traces of the forts and camps of Celtic Britons, who witnessed the arrival of a great civilisation from Rome. The Romans' finest treasure, which was only rediscovered in 1879, must be the baths at Aquae Sulis, a remarkably well preserved complex that provides a fascinating insight into both their mastery of technology and the comfortable lifestyle they enjoyed. Less dramatic, perhaps, but equally impressive aspects of their culture are expressed in the other towns and villas they founded in northern Somerset and, of course, the many roads they laid, the most well known being the Fosse Way.

In the wake of those soldiers came traders, among whom is said to have been Joseph of Arimathea, traditionally believed to have brought the young boy Jesus and the first Christianity to these shores. He landed near what is now Glastonbury, and from his staff, thrust into a hillside, the holy flowering thorn sprouted. Joseph founded a church, where the ruins of the great abbey now lie, and buried the holy chalice by a spring issuing from the base of the Tor, whose waters reputedly have healing properties. Whether the stories have credence or not, Christianity did first arrive during the Roman period, from which grew a great Celtic tradition that remained a strong, if isolated, spiritual force until it eventually conceded to the papal missionaries of a later Rome.

Much of the legacy of the powerful Roman civilisation was lost when the Empire collapsed, a void which Germanic tribes were quick to exploit. But the Saxon advance was halted, for a while at least, by a Celtic warrior whose charismatic leadership won victory on Mount Badon. Although the site is now lost, the conquest is associated with the legendary King Arthur, whose court, some believe, lay on a hill above South Cadbury. More tangible is a later hero, Alfred the Great, who although demonstrating ineptitude as a baker, showed other talents in raising a force in Somerset, which was sufficient to defend his kingdom of Wessex from the Vikings in 878. In time the Normans came, and a great era of church building followed, often reworking ancient sites with their Gothic masterpieces, a celebration of faith in stone that has produced an abundance of churches, whose finest rank with the best in the country.

Although the Civil Wars affected this part of the

country less than most, the later rebellion against the Crown, led by the Duke of Monmouth, was to rock the countryside. His brief foray was brought to a halt at the Battle of Sedgemoor in 1685, the last to be fought on English soil. The aftermath was perhaps even more terrible, as retribution followed and many were hanged, deported or imprisoned for the support they had given to the hapless duke.

Interwoven in this history are the lives of the ordinary people, those who had a living to make from the land on which they lived. And it is from the land that Somerset's wealth has been won. From Saxon times, the hills and pastures have been grazed by sheep, whose fleeces were the raw material for an industry that was to prosper for centuries. It was the profits from woollen cloth that founded the great monasteries and raised the many elegant church towers for which the county is famed. Also significant was mining, and lead, whose ore was dug from the Mendips by the Romans, was traded throughout their Empire. Coal too became important as the industrial age gathered momentum, and the type found in Somerset, around Radstock and Pensford, with its high bituminous content, was particularly suitable for the production of coal gas and coke.

Many of the old industries have gone, despite the building of railways and canals, victims of geographical remoteness and lack of immediate access to the power resources required by the intensive productive machinery of a new age. More recently there has been some diversity into light technology and commerce, however, agriculture remains a mainstay of the economy, with some 80% of the county being devoted to it in one form or another.

One of today's main sources of both employment and income is tourism, something that has roots well back in history. Even in medieval times, Glastonbury drew its crowds, pilgrims, eager to tread the very ground on which Jesus had walked. As now, they needed food and accommodation and everyone sought that all-important memento to take with them as they returned home. In 1191, when trade began to flag, the ever-enterprising monks made a miraculous discovery. They found the bones of Arthur and Guinevere, relics which helped assure the abbey's economic future and even drew a king and queen to witness their reburial. Today, Glastonbury is still a focus for Christian religious pilgrimage, but with the wealth of myth and legend associated with it, the town has also come to be regarded by some as the mystical centre of England. Disciples of 'New Age' cults are attracted from the four corners of the country, and each year thousands head for the famous Glastonbury Festival held at nearby Pilton.

Modern tourism, however, can perhaps be traced back to the beginning of the 18th century with the appointment of the dandy Richard 'Beau' Nash as Master of Ceremonies to the spa resort of Bath. Although attracting a steady stream of visitors over

the centuries, seeking relief from the curative properties of its waters, the city had become so dirty and infested that the afflicted were in danger of exchanging one disease for another, infinitely more deadly. Nash set to work cleaning up the place, and success followed almost immediately, attracting not only the leading socialites of the day, but also men of ideas and resource. Their investment created a city that is now regarded as one of the finest architectural achievements of its age and Bath continues to rank as one of the most popular destinations for visitors in Britain.

The fashion for cures was also exploited along the coast, with resorts developing to meet the growing popularity for seawater treatments. It did not take long for people to realise that the 'cure' need not necessarily be vile to be effective, and that a trip to the sea could be a pleasurable experience, provided one refrained from actually drinking it. The air at Weston was considered to be particularly beneficial, and it rapidly emerged as a leading resort, aided by the railways and its proximity by steamer to the mining towns of South Wales. While Weston and its neighbours, such as Clevedon and Portishead, are still popular today, the rest of the county, too, has much to offer in the discovery and enjoyment of its beautiful countryside and attractive villages.

The pictures in this book, which span a period from the end of the 19th to the middle of the 20th centuries, are a history, not of the great or momentous events of time, but more the minutiae of daily activity. The book is an ideal introduction to an exploration of Somerset's towns, villages and countryside, where everywhere you will find relics and clues that help illuminate its fascinating past. These photographs show that the process of change is ever-continuing and allow a point of reference for, or comparison with, what has happened since they were taken. In some, occasionally even those of the earliest era, the change is surprisingly superficial and the scene little different to that which exists today. But in others, the transformation is dramatic, making it almost impossible to reconcile the past view with the present. What is obvious is that the greatest changes seem to have been wrought within the last 30 or 40 years, within the lifetimes of many who will read this book.

Bath
The Abbey and Pump Room 1929 82332
Ironically, Bath's prominence as a fashionable spa town during the 18th century was achieved without any inkling of what lay beneath the pavements - the baths. The Pump Room, completed in 1796, was where the sick and the socialites came to 'take the waters'. The abbey was founded in the 9th century, but the present building was not begun until 1499.

Around Bath and the Avon Tributaries

Bath
The Roman Baths 1897
40789
Legend attributes the discovery of the hot spring's curative powers to Prince Bladud, who found himself cured of leprosy. Although probably already sacred to the Celts, it was the Romans who first truly exploited the site by building Aquae Sulis. But, after the Romans left, the baths became covered with mud and were not rediscovered until 1879.

Bath
Cavendish Crescent 1907 57717
The appointment of Beau Nash as 'Master of Ceremonies' heralded Bath's rebirth. He improved its squalid conditions and attracted others with the means and vision to create an elegant city. The John Woods - father and son - were responsible for much of the new city's architecture and it was the inspiration of John the Younger that conceived magnificent crescents such as this.

▼ **Bath, Great Pulteney Street 1890** 25130
Named after William Pulteney, Earl of Bath, and designed by Thomas Baldwin, this has been described as the finest street in Europe. Pictured in winter, a dusting of snow covers the ground and carriage drivers await a summons to take residents into town. The horses are gone and the fountain has changed, but otherwise the street looks just the same today.

▲ **Bath, Union Street 1923** 73964
The stern-looking traffic policeman would not be employed today as the street has now been pedestrianised. 30 years on from photograph 36457, there is not a horse-drawn vehicle in sight and apart from most men wearing hats, male dress fashions here do not appear all that dated.

▼ **Bath, Milsom Street 1895** 36457
An assortment of shops lines the road, which looks towards George Street. Here we can see evidence of just how much clothing fashions have changed. The girl in the foreground wears a straw hat and long dress with voluminous sleeves. A boy to the right wears knickerbockers and a high-buttoned jacket, while the gentleman outside Lipton's grocers sports a top hat and cape.

Bath
The Old Bridge 1887

19590

The Old Bridge across the Avon was built in 1754 and incorporated an earlier bridge from the 14th century. Sadly it was demolished and replaced in 1966 by a modern road bridge. The crenellated arches in the background follow the line of the old Roman walls and carry Brunel's railway to the city station, just to the left.

Charlcombe,The Church 1907 57754
Dedicated to St Mary the Virgin, this beautiful, tiny church still seems far from the heart of the city that lies barely two miles away at the foot of the hill. Constructed of local limestone, the Victorians rebuilt much of its ancient fabric and, more recently, fine oak pews from the Robert Thompson workshops in Yorkshire have been installed.

Swainswick, The Brook c1955 S272006
Although the corner shops have now closed, the row of houses climbing the hill, Otago Terrace, is little changed since the photograph was taken. The dilapidated footbridge over Lam Brook has now been repaired, but the site of the cottage just behind it is now occupied by a children's playground.

Batheaston, The Weir 1907 57751
Just below Batheaston village, a weir impedes the progress of the Avon, serving to impound water to power two mills. The one shown here on the far bank once manufactured gunpowder and the other, on the northern bank, was used to grind corn. Both are still there today, but have been converted into hotels.

Batheaston, The Weir c1960 B308013
50 years on from photograph 57751, the old gunpowder mill is shown in its new role, the Weir Tea Garden Hotel. Pleasant gardens line the river-bank, where guests relaxed on hot summer days over their afternoon tea, reclining in deckchairs under the shade of parasols, lulled by the sound of water splashing over the weir.

Batheaston, The Bridge and Weir 1907 57750
Seen from the opposite bank of the river, this fine arched bridge was built to serve a livestock market at neighbouring Bathampton. The toll-house, hidden by trees on the left, still carries a board detailing the charges once levied; a score of pigs or sheep cost the same as a car, 6d, while cattle and people were each charged ½d.

Batheaston, High Street c1960 B308018
Although more traffic now passes along the street, its character has changed little over the last 40 years. The Post Office is still there, although the post box on the wall has been changed. The bakers, next door but one, has gone, but its 'Hovis' sign still decorates the wall.

Batheaston St Catherine's Court c1960 B308035
Reached by a narrow lane through a peaceful valley above the town, St Catherine's Court stands on the site of a 13th-century monastery, once occupied by monks from Bath Abbey. The church, whose tower rises behind the house, contains a fine memorial to William Blanchard and his family, who purchased the property at the end of the 16th century.

Bathford
Brown's Folly c1955
B309002
Occupying a commanding position on Bathford Hill, this 19th-century tower enjoys a superb view across the Avon Valley. The slopes were mined for limestone from Roman times until the early 20th century, and abandoned entrances lie hidden by vegetation. During World War II, they served as an ammunition store but today are an important habitat for many species of bats.

◄ **Bathford**
The Crown Inn c1955
B309008

Lying at the foot of a steep hill rising into the village, the Crown overlooks a 17th-century bridge across one of the Avon's tributaries. Buses still stop outside the inn, and at one time trams too ran here from the nearby city of Bath.

Bathford
Church Street c1955
B309005
Looking away from St Swithun's Church, where lies buried the body of Lord Admiral Nelson's sister, Ann, this view has changed little during the last half century. The massive stone cylinder, lying by the first house, was a field roller and would have been drawn by a carthorse. Notice too, on the opposite side, a cast-iron drinking fountain.

Bathampton
The Canal and George Inn 1907 57749
Washing lines suggest a Monday morning view along the Kennet and Avon Canal, which was conceived in 1794 to link the Thames and Bristol Channel. The waterway quickly became a great success and, in its heyday, annually carried some 350,000 tons of freight. However, the railways heralded its decline and it was taken over by the Great Western Railway.

Monkton Combe
The School Chapel c1955
M126003
The school was founded in 1868 by the village's vicar and among its former pupils are two Olympic medal winners, William Laurie (1948) and Rowley Douglas (2000), who both achieved gold in rowing. Its chapel has been recently extended to accommodate an increasing number of pupils, and carries the school's motto, 'Verbum Tuum Veritas', and crest above its door.

Monkton Combe, The Village c1955 M126020

Partly obscured at the bottom of Mill Lane, the oddly-roofed stone building, erected in 1776, once served the village as its lock-up. The street acquired fame in 1952 when it was used as a location for the classic Ealing comedy 'The Titfield Thunderbolt'. Monkton Station became Titfield and the commuters walked along Mill Lane to catch the train.

Monkton Combe, The Viaduct c1955 M126021

The A36 between Warminster and Bath crosses the deep Midford Brook valley and the Somerset - Wiltshire border on this impressive many-arched viaduct. Beneath it ran the railway, although by the time of this photograph, the line had already ceased to operate. Its course is now followed by a footpath, and the open fields form part of Monkton's playing fields.

Hinton Charterhouse The Village c1965

H165002

Straddling a Roman road, Hinton lies close to the ruins of a Carthusian priory. The village centre buildings, constructed of local stone, are outwardly little changed, though visitors today will find that The Crown has now added a Rose to its name and the creeper adorning the Malt House has now been removed, exposing its clean-lined 18th-century façade.

Wellow
The Village c1955
W180003

The local school, which is still used as such, was built in 1852 and stands part way along on the right. The village also had several dairy farms and the churn, just visible behind the little girl, has been left there for collection after the milking. The protruding extension on the house opposite accommodated both a bread oven and well.

Wellow, St Julian's Church c1955 W180005
The dedication to a Roman saint and a nearby Roman villa suggest that this has been a Christian site since before 400AD. The present church, built in the Perpendicular style around 1370, is closely connected with the Hungerfords, who then owned the manor. The family chapel contains fine 15th-century frescoes and an impressive painted 17th-century tomb memorial.

Norton St Philip, The George Inn c1950 N218001
Little changed over the centuries, the origins of the George Inn lie in a hostel, built about 1250 as a guest house for nearby Hinton Priory, when the village was an important centre for wool production. Among its visitors have been the Duke of Monmouth, who survived an assassination attempt here, and Samuel Pepys, who dined well on 10 shillings.

Norton St Philip, High Street c1955 N218015
Winding streets fronted by characterful stone cottages of different periods typify this attractive village. The Ebenezer Chapel was built in 1814, at a time when many working-class people, disillusioned with the established Church and its teachings, looked to the non-conformist religions for both their spiritual and practical guidance.

Radstock, The Valley and Railway 1914 66584
In the 19th and early 20th centuries, Radstock was an important coal-mining town and was serviced by two separate railways, the Somerset and Dorset, later incorporated within the London, Midland, Scottish railway (shown to the left), and the Great Western. The building fronting the LMS line was the town's market hall and now houses the fascinating Radstock Museum.

KILMERSDON 2

Radstock
The Level Crossing and Station c1955

R2004

Although the Bell Hotel remains, the two level crossings, station buildings and platforms have now disappeared. The last passenger traffic on the LMS was carried in 1959 and on the GWR in 1966. The site in front of the market hall is now an open space and a colliery wheel has been erected as a reminder of the town's past.

▼ **Radstock, Wells Hill 1914** 66587

Life in England was very different at the start of the Great War. Travelling knife-grinders moved between villages, and deliveries and passenger transport generally relied on horsepower rather than motor vehicles. The building on the left, built in 1874, houses the local Co-operative Society, which was founded in 1868, and looks across to a newly-planted sapling oak.

▼ **Radstock, The Centre c1960** R2025

Nearly 50 years on from photograph 66587 and looking the other way, the tip of the oak tree is just identifiable on the right. The Co-operative Society has now expanded, and has built a large store opposite its original headquarters, both of which, incidentally, the company continues to occupy under its new trading name, 'Radco'.

▲ **Radstock Victoria Hall c1955** R2003

First erected in 1866 by Countess Waldegrave as a miners' recreation and reading room, it was enlarged to incorporate a dance hall in 1897 to commemorate Queen Victoria's Diamond Jubilee. The war memorial opposite remembers the town's sacrifice in two world wars. Behind can be seen Ludlow's colliery, which closed in 1954.

Midsomer Norton High Street 1952 M125005
Half a century ago, High Street contained a varied collection of small, family-run shops, with signboards advertising their presence. Large hoardings encouraged housewives to buy products such as the floor polish, advertised here, but unlike today's billboards, these were painted or metal signs and not papered over with a new advert almost every week.

Midsomer Norton, High Street c1965 M125018
This row of shops, opposite the Town Hall, has perhaps altered less during the last 40 years than many other parts of High Street, and the different building styles from the 18th and 19th centuries add interest to the view. The bank and Casswells are still there today, although the other shops now serve different trades.

Midsomer Norton, The Island c1965 M125019
The industrial buildings in the background housed an agricultural mill producing animal foodstuffs, while the shop in front, Don Scammell, sold carpets. Opposite, the White Hart remains instantly recognisable today, but the building next door, advertising 'Lyons Tea', which was once Mr Edwards' Café, has since been rendered and now serves as an opticians.

Kilmersdon, The Manor House c1960 K181011
Built in 1664, the older part of the Manor House has fine mullioned windows set in two outward-facing gables. An extension, probably added during the 18th century, demonstrates a confident prosperity and a desire for greater comfort, expressed in larger rooms and airy windows.

Kilmersdon, The Church c1960 K181013
The village is centred on its church, dedicated to Saints Peter and Paul. Externally, the building is decorated with many carvings, among which are a king, queen and ferocious animals, and the niches on the tower once accommodated statues of saints. To the right, the Jolliffe Arms is the village pub and also served as the manor courtroom.

▼ **Farleigh Hungerford, The Castle and Castle House c1955** F219054
Castle House lies beside a quiet lane running between the river and millstream towards the foot of the still imposing castle enclosure. Originally a manor house, the fortifications were raised by Sir Thomas Hungerford in 1370. He held office as the first Speaker of the House of Commons, a position also held by his son, Sir Walter.

▼ **Farleigh Hungerford, The Castle 1907** 57756
Originally overlooking a ditch, the gatehouse incorporated a wide drawbridge, which, when raised, fitted within the recess surrounding the entrance arch. Hidden by creepers, above the window, is the carved crest of the Hungerfords, who lived here for two centuries. In 1907, the buildings to the right served as a dairy, and a milk cart and churns stand outside.

▲ **Frome Market Place c1965**
F58080
Pronounced 'froom', like the river on which it lies, the town's recorded history begins in 685 when St Aldhelm founded a monastery. One Wessex king, Athelstan, held his Council here, while another, Edred, died here. In 1685, Monmouth passed a night in the town, but later, 12 inhabitants who had shown sympathy to his cause were hanged in the Market Place.

Frome
Market Place c1965

F58059

Frome was once a busy market town, so much so that it could support two hotels, the George and the Crown. The market cross, which rises above a now-disused water fountain, was donated by Richard Cavendish Boyle in 1871 and is inscribed with his entwined initials. The policeman seemingly dancing a jig in the road is actually guiding three children across.

Frome, Bath Street 1907 58845
The imposing building to the left is Rook Lane Chapel, which was built in 1707 and bears the inscription 'Keep thy foot when thou goest to the House of God'. The attractive cottages look much the same a century later, although their railings have disappeared, quite possibly in response to a national appeal for scrap metal during World War II.

Frome, Willow Vale 1907 58849
A quiet riverside haven off the main road, the buildings on the right housed livery stables. From the 14th century, the river served prosperous wool and dying industries, and often flowed red and blue as a result. Metal casting superseded their decline in the 19th century - Bodicea's statue in London was made in Frome.

Frome, Welsh Mill Bridge 1907 58860

The Frome has often over-spilled its course through the town, and as a result of efforts to contain its passage, this scene no longer exists. The river has been diverted some 50 yards left and is now spanned by a utilitarian concrete bridge. The original riverbed has been filled in and is occupied by a children's play area.

Mells, Woodlands End c1955 M56016

The village shop, advertising 'Lyons Tea', was an indispensable focus for the community, and stocked an incredible range of basic commodities. Opposite, by a stream out of picture, is an unusual stone triangular shelter, designed by Sir Edward Lutyens in memory of Mark Horner who died in 1908. Apparently, the village washerwomen used to gather to do their work there.

Mells, The Manor and Church c1965 M56037
John Horner acquired the manor after the Dissolution, although there is no factual support that he stole the deeds while carrying them to the King from the Abbot of Glastonbury, who had hoped the gift would appease Henry and thus save the abbey. The estate has now passed by marriage to the Asquith family.

Mells, The Green c1965 M56038
Lying on the hillside at the top of the village, the attractive cottage shown here adjoins another that once housed the local forge. Apart from shoeing horses, the blacksmith had to be accomplished in making and repairing a whole range of articles, from spades and ploughs to hinges and springs.

Nunney The Village and Castle 1907 58877
Behind the village, the remains of Nunney's 14th-century castle are softened by overgrowing vegetation. At the far end of the street stands The George Inn, named after England's patron saint. Unusually, its sign hangs below an arched beam that completely spans the road. An old coaching inn, an archway leads through to an enclosed courtyard.

Nunney
The Village and Castle
1907 58876

Sir John de la Mare built his castle in the French style having just returned from the wars there in 1373. Held for the Royalists during the Civil Wars, it finally surrendered after a lengthy siege, during which the inmates daily tormented their only pig to give the impression they had ample supplies and slaughtered a fresh animal each day.

Nunney, from the Bridge 1907 58879
All Saints Church, in the background, dates from the 13th century, although a fragment of Saxon cross suggesting evidence of an earlier building is displayed in the chancel. Inside are several interesting recumbent effigies and a beautifully carved screen across the chancel arch. In medieval times the stream was used for washing woollen cloth, produced in the village.

Keynsham, High Street 1950 K64003
Most signs of Keynsham's history are not now immediately obvious. Roman villas and a 12th-century abbey have disappeared without trace and a brass industry, which rose to prominence during the 18th century, had gone by 1927. Although the shop fronts have been 'modernised' and there is considerably more traffic, this view appears substantially the same today.

Keynsham, The Parish Church c1950 K64007
At the top of Bristol Road is St John the Baptist's Parish Church. It dates from the 13th century and, inside, contains some impressive tomb monuments. The tower, however, is more recent, having been rebuilt following a lightning strike in 1632. The debris crashed through the roof of the nave, demolishing the chancel screen.

Keynsham, The River Chew c1960 K64019
One of the town's brass mills stood here, just beyond the weir. Part of Keynsham's park, the site is now occupied by a small picnic area. The bridge from which the photograph was taken was later washed away when, on 10 July 1968, four inches of rain fell in seven hours, turning the river into a torrent.

Keynsham, The County Bridge from the River Chew c1960 K64024
Crossing the Avon, just below its confluence with the Chew, the bridge linked Somerset and Gloucestershire. During Monmouth's Rebellion, it was breached to frustrate the Duke's advance, but was repaired and lived on until its final destruction during the terrible flood of 10 July 1968. Nothing remains of its fine arches, and its replacement is a plain, utilitarian span.

Pensford, High Street c1955 P140004
Once a coal town, this attractive row of russet-coloured stone cottages housed the miners who worked underground. Towards the bottom, set back on the right, is the George and Dragon, an old coaching inn whose archway leads to a yard at the rear. Nearby is an old stone lock-up, built in the 18th century and a fine example of its type.

Pensford, The Village c1955 P140012
At the bottom of the town runs the River Chew and, just visible in front of the church, is the old road-bridge. The viaduct behind was built in 1873 and carried the Somerset and Dorset line north to Bristol until it closed in 1959. Still going strong, however, is the town's most famous son, Aker Bilk, the jazz musician.

▼ **Pensford, General View c1955** P140005
The main road to Bristol sweeps through the lower town, carried over the Chew by a modern bridge that superseded the narrow bridge by the church. The new road bridge was swept away in 1968 and, during the construction of its replacement, traffic once again relied on the old bridge.

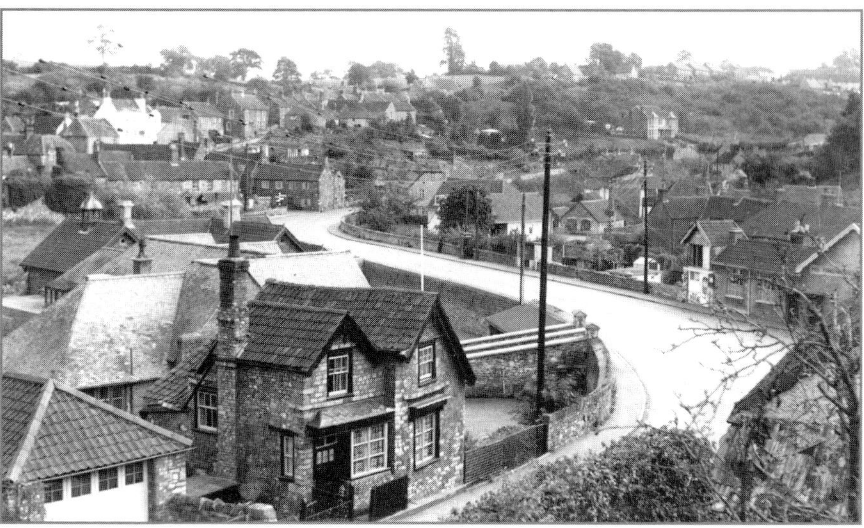

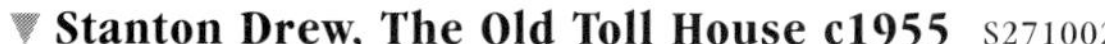

▼ **Stanton Drew, The Old Toll House c1955** S271002
This unusual tiny round building, which stands at the head of the lane into the village, was built in the 15th century and later used as a toll-house when the turnpike was opened in 1790. It stands there much the same today, with its small outhouse now also covered in thatch.

▲ **Chew Magna The Corner Shop c1965** C230028
In Tudor times, the place was well established in the wool industry, manufacturing cloth and stockings. It also produced reddle, a red dye used by shepherds to mark their sheep. A distinctive feature of the village is its elevated pavements, here emphasised by the parked Morris Minor estate car, something pedestrians must have been grateful for before the roads were paved.

Chew Magna
South Parade c1955

C230003

The bus arrives on its journey to Bristol, a service still running today, and a lady with a young child stands outside the village shop. At the bottom of the street, by the Westminster Bank, stands the church ale house, built in the early 1500s. Ale brewed there was sold on feast and fair days, the profits going to the church.

Bishop Sutton, The Red Lion c1955 B310003
This smart looking Ford Popular, which then cost £390, was perhaps the photographer's pride and joy, and stands conspicuously on the Red Lion's deserted forecourt. The building behind the pub was originally a mill, part of which was later demolished to allow for a road improvement scheme. Today, evidence of its former use lies in millstones embedded in the wall.

Bishop Sutton, Chew Valley Lake c1955 B310016
Lying west of the village is the Chew Valley reservoir. Although planned in the early 1930s, construction was delayed by the war. The photograph, taken shortly before its inauguration by the Queen in 1956, looks out from Knowle Hill to Denny Island. The lake covers some 486 hectares and attracts many species of both breeding and migrant birds.

The Mendips and Beyond

Hutton, The Village c1965 H166008
Taken outside the village school, which was built in 1876 for £850, the photograph looks along the narrow main street between the old Post Office and Old Post Office Farm, past white-painted cottages. There is now a pavement and, although some of the cottages have gone, the old village pump is still to be found by the road.

Banwell, West Street c1960 B307018
The boulder outside the chemist is known as the 'butstone', and gave the building its name. Exactly what it was, or when it first appeared, has been lost in time, but popular opinion suggests it was a mounting block, a function which it certainly served during the early part of the 20th century, when Butstone House was a tack shop.

Loxton, Crook Peak c1965 L149002

This view is an almost timeless scene across green fields from the hamlet of Loxton to the distinctively-shaped summit of Crook Peak. It rises above the Lox Yeo River, whose course is marked by the line of trees in the middle of the photograph. The view today would include the M5 motorway, following a line above the river, close to the pylon.

Winscombe, Woodborough Road c1965 W183034

This view towards the former railway station looks much the same today. However, there were no yellow lines then, and cars were able to park conveniently outside the shops; the Mini and Morris Minor were popular models of the day. Brown's grocery shop has a fine display of tins in its window, and prices advertised in pre-decimalisation shillings and pence.

Churchill, The Clock Tower c1955 C231022
Standing beside a small triangular garden, the Clock Tower was commissioned in 1897 by Sidney Hill to commemorate Victoria's Diamond Jubilee. An oak tree, set in a circular railed enclosure outside the village pub, the Nelson's Arms, was also planted to mark the occasion. A local philanthropist, Hill applied much of his wealth to the benefit of the community.

Compton Martin, The Post Office c1955 C233002
This delightful view has changed little during the last half century, and ducks still dabble on the pond while fish, some almost two feet in length, swim lazily to and fro. Standing beside the main road through the village, the local store and post office remains a focal point in the community.

West Harptree
The Village c1965
W181019
Built of red stone, the cottages lining the road here move back to make room for a junction in the centre of the village. Some have their fronts opened as shop windows, and one, towards the far end, also serves as a filling station. The village pub continues today, but the old-style red telephone box outside has gone.

West Harptree
The Village c1965 W181046

Looking the opposite way towards the village store and filling station, we can see that it also sold bottled gas, something common before mains supplies were generally available outside the larger towns. The building on the left is described as the 'Old Bakery', but the shops in that row have now gone, leaving only a beauty salon at the very end.

East Harptree, The Clock c1965 E65007

Erected at the head of the High Street in June 1897, this clock, with its rather ornate roof, commemorates the 60th year of Queen Victoria's reign. As ever, seizing the opportunity to preach religious and moral guidance, the benefactors adorned their monument with the inscriptions 'Heaven's light our guide' and 'Time flies don't delay'.

DAIRY UTENSIL MANUFACTORY.
TO THE

Shepton Mallet Town Street 1899

44543

Shepton's streets have been busy with trade ever since the Romans established a settlement by the Fosse Way. Victorian traders, keen to attract custom, display their wares; waterproof coats and trousers, milk jugs and a festoon of boots and shoes, are some of the things instantly recognisable. The photographer has attracted attention too, even the postman has stopped to watch.

Doulting
The Church 1899 44101
Tradition holds that St Aldhelm died here in 709, close by a wooden church he had himself founded. More substantial buildings followed, culminating in the present church, which, although extensively restored in 1869, derives from a 15th-century rebuilding. To the west, down a quiet lane is St Aldhelm's well, a natural spring where he is said to have bathed.

Bruton, View from the Dovecote c1960 B842009
Taken from beside a 16th-century dovecote, once part of an Augustinian priory and one of the National Trust's first acquisitions, the view overlooks the railway to St Mary's Church. The town was an important Saxon burgh with its own mint. Later prosperity came from wool and then silk production and the town is still noted for its several fine schools.

Bruton, High Street c1955 B842010

A multiformity of buildings, each snuggled against its neighbour, attractively line both sides of the street. On the right, narrow alleyways pierce the façade and lead down past long, walled gardens to the river behind. The building at the far end is the town's library, while the shop by the parked van has long been a pharmacy.

Bruton, The Packhorse Bridge c1955 B842016

Providing a dry passage across the Brue between the monastery buildings on the right and the town, is this fine 15th-century packhorse bridge. The photograph was taken from a row of ancient stepping stones, which it superseded. The building on the right is part of King's School, originally founded by the monastic order in 1519.

Castle Cary, The Church from Lodge Hill c1955 C611017

Looking onto the town from Lodge Hill, All Saint's Church captures the eye. To the left, a bellcote rises from the village school, founded in 1876 and typical of many of its era. Water from the pond feeds another in the town, where sits the island war memorial and nearby stood an 11th-century castle, of which nothing visible remains.

Castle Cary, The Market Place c1960 C611045

The striking arcaded building in the centre of the square was the Market Hall. Originally erected in 1616, it was rebuilt in 1855 and now serves as the town's information centre and museum. Deserted streets and the time suggest early morning, and some of the cars perhaps belong to guests staying at the George Hotel opposite.

Castle Cary The George Hotel c1955 C611013

With a thatched roof and intricate wrought iron bracket that would normally carry its sign, the George Hotel is over four centuries old. Further down the street, a 'Regent' sign advertises a petrol station amongst the row of shops. Opposite is Barclays Bank, which is still there today, but an antique dealer now occupies The Angel Hotel.

Castle Cary
The Old Prison c1955
C611023

In the centre of a small square on Bailey Hill is the town's lock-up, built in 1779 for the princely sum of £23. Once a common feature in England's towns and villages, few now remain. The fine Georgian façade behind houses the town's Post Office, and to the left, but out of the picture, is a former rope factory.

Wincanton, Market Place c1965 W599102

Formerly a wool town, Wincanton emerged during the 18th century as an important coach halt on the London - Exeter road. Much of High Street was rebuilt during that period, following a devastating fire in 1747, leaving a legacy of fine Georgian buildings. The Bear was one of the 'new' coaching inns, its archway leading to stabling behind.

Wincanton, the White Horse Hotel c1960 W599092

Further up the hill on the opposite side, the White Horse Hotel was also a coaching inn. Although of a similar period, its appearance is strikingly different to The Bear. The stone work has not been rendered and protruding keystones and quoins emphasise the windows and corners of the building.

Wincanton The Clock c1960
W599073

Dominating the Market Place and rising above the town's library is an imposing clock tower, which was rebuilt in 1878 in the distinctive style often adopted for civic architecture of the period. Other users of the building are Wincanton Men's Club, entered by the open door at its base and The Clock Café, around the corner.

Milborne Port The Village 1959 M180005
Remote from the sea, its name describes not a harbour, but its status as a market town on a millstream. Indeed, there were once several mills and the people made their living producing leather, flax, grain and wool. Dominating the scene is the 18th-century Town Hall, adorned with a large clock and topped by a bellcote.

Pilton
The Church and Village c1960 P383054
2,000 years ago, the village had a harbour, and legend tells that Joseph of Arimathea brought Jesus here while trading for lead, and founded a small church. The present Norman building, dedicated to St John the Baptist, is held to be on the same site, making it one of the oldest places of Christian worship in the country.

Milborne Port
The Village 1959 M180006
Although set back from the road, the King's Head is identifiable from its name board. However, to find it today, it would be necessary to search out 'The Tippling Philosopher'. Missed by the photographer, just to the left is the ancient Guildhall, whose entrance is decorated with fine Norman carving taken from nearby St John's Church.

Pilton
The Post Office c1955
P383019
By the Crown Inn, the window of the village store and post office is packed with an astonishing variety of both goods and displays, advertising everything from pipe tobacco to baby medicines and oxtail soup to an Araby beauty course. Behind the low wall on the right, originally a cattle pound, was a tree planted to commemorate Victoria's Diamond Jubilee.

Wells
The Cathedral, West Front 1923 73993
St Aldhelm founded the church in the early 8th century, near a spring from which the city takes its name. Although there has been a cathedral here since 909, the present edifice was not begun until 1180. Building spanned some four centuries and this magnificently ornate west front was only completed around 1235, the towers taking another 200 years.

Wells, The Cathedral, Choir East 1890 23883

The choir was amongst the earlier parts of the cathedral to be completed but was considerably altered during the 14th century. Clusters of slender columns disguise the bulk of its massive piers, and rise into splendid pointed arches. Beyond is the retro-choir, built to house the relics of Bishop de la Marchia, which stands empty as the attempt to elevate him to sainthood failed.

Wells, The Bishop's Palace 1890 23895

Set behind battlemented walls and surrounded by a moat fed by the resurgent waters, the palace was begun by Bishop Jocelin in the 13th century. Added to by his successors over the next two centuries, it served as the Bishop's official residence. Set amid peaceful grounds, the ruins and other buildings, still used today, are a haven from the city outside.

Wells Market Place c1965 W47097

The magnificent gatehouse, erected in the 15th century by Bishop Bekynton, leads to the Bishop's Palace and is known as the Bishop's Eye. The Crown Hotel is a 15th-century coaching inn, and from here in 1685, the Quaker, William Penn, who went on to found Pennsylvania, addressed a massive crowd, for which he was subsequently arrested.

Priddy
The Green c1960 P385006
This photograph was taken just before the famous Sheep Fair, which takes place on the Wednesday nearest 21 August. Originally held at Wells, the fair moved to Priddy in 1348 when the Black Death broke out. The thatch protects the hurdles used for pens, although to avoid dismantling it, others are brought in annually for the event.

Priddy
The Pool c1960 P385012
The village is the highest in Somerset, and during the Middle Ages, the surrounding area was mined for lead. A mile to the east lie Priddy Pools, an unusual phenomena created by a stratum of impermeable sandstone overlying the limestone hills. It is now a designated nature reserve and in summer, an attractive leisure spot.

Cheddar, Jacob's Ladder 1910 62252
A spectacular road winds from the Mendip plateau through one of England's finest natural formations, Cheddar Gorge. At the bottom, enclosed by cliffs almost 450 feet high, lie its most famous attractions, the caves. A tower at the top of Jacob's Ladder, here viewed from near Lion's Rock opposite, gives the best view of the gorge.

Cheddar, Lion Rock 1890 27867A
In 1873 George Cox discovered the first cave and, quickly seeing its potential, enlarged the entrance to open it as a show cavern. Although by the time of this photograph, it was already a noted attraction, the entrance to the gorge has not yet lost its natural charm. The pool, fed by resurgent streams, then supplied a mill.

Cheddar, Entrance to Pass 1908 60134
20 years on from photograph 27867A, gift shops have begun to make their appearance, selling souvenirs and post cards to the spellbound tourists. Even the King had graced the cavern with his presence and the French spelaeologist, E A Martel, who pioneered the exploration of many of his country's caves, regarded it as the finest he had ever seen.

Cheddar, The Entrance to Cox's Cavern 1925 77552
Tourism has now really caught on, but with car travel still in its infancy, a hotel was needed to provide overnight accommodation for visitors. Porters wait outside to receive guests and signs advertise the hostelry's recommendation by the RAC, AA and ACU, the Auto-Cycle Union. Then called The Cliff, dinner and bed for the night cost only 11 shillings.

Axbridge High Street c1955 A254016

During Saxon times, it was a walled town with a mint. Axbridge is one of few places in England still feeling medieval and, behind their overhanging, rendered façades, many buildings are timber-framed. A hand-operated BP pump, dispensing petrol at 1s 5d per gallon, marks a garage and cycle shop, and meat hooks hang above the window of the butcher's shop opposite.

Cheddar
Cox's Cave c1955
C71037
Although the gorge is now heavily commercialised, the natural formations within the caves are among the most spectacular that are readily accessible in this country, and remain the focal point of any visit. Innumerable stalactites and stalagmites, concretions and pools, create breathtaking sights dramatically enhanced by mystical effects of light and shadow.

Axbridge
Market Place c1955
A254018
Narrow streets open into the central square, which is dominated here by The Lamb Hotel. It was a coaching inn during the 18th century. Note the rounded stone block by the entrance to the courtyard, placed there to protect the wall from collision as coaches passed through. The George Hotel has now closed and the premises are occupied by estate agents.

Axbridge
King John's Hunting Lodge c1960 A254025
Popularly known as King John's Hunting Lodge, this building was probably a Tudor merchant's house. However, links lie in King John granting certain rights to the town, and the surrounding area was a hunting ground for both Saxon and Norman kings. More recently, the timber frame of the building has been exposed and it now houses an interesting museum.

Brooke
Bond
Tea
CITY
HEWETTS
635 MHT
LYONS

Around the Kenn and Yeo

Nailsea, High Street c1965 N65036
In 1974, the centre of Nailsea was completely redeveloped to create a new shopping area, and this and the following photograph are now all but unrecognisable. Looking along High Street from the green, the Queen's Head on the right is the only building of those in the foreground still standing, although some shops and houses at the far end survive.

Nailsea, The Post Office and Green c1965 N65018
This oak is the only remaining feature, planted in 1897 for Victoria's Diamond Jubilee. That it escaped the developer's destructive scheme is perhaps due to its growing on ground gifted to the parish by Mrs Fanny Russell. Even that was not sacrosanct, and the pleasant shady spot shown here has been reshaped and planted with shrubbery.

Farleigh, The Old School House c1955 F70001
The thatch on this delightfully picturesque old cottage ripples gracefully over the two upper windows that illuminate its attic rooms. Sadly, much of the building has since been demolished, and a blank-walled façade now looks down the street. As if to compensate, the adjacent Victorian gothic gable has been restored, and the bellcote still crowns the apex.

Farleigh, Old Cottages c1955 F70003

Farleigh Cottage, built in the 17th century, is another cottage off the main road opposite the George Inn. Although the climbing plants that adorned its walls have now been removed, the thatch remains, and flows over the upper storey windows. Although now little used, thatch was a readily obtainable and practical roofing material that helped insulate the building.

Backwell, West Town c1955 B564024

A signboard identifies the Rising Sun and, set back from the road and on the opposite side, is the New Inn, each pub selling the beer of a different local brewery. The billboard is advertising 'Chivers Jellies' and 'Guinness'. The famous toucan, which is partly obscured, first appeared in 1935, with a caption written by the crime writer Dorothy L Sayers.

Yatton, High Street c1955 Y47015
Yatton developed in the mid-19th century around an important railway junction. Trains still operate along the line from Bristol to Bridgwater and beyond, but the other track, which wound around the southern edge of the Mendips to Wells has gone. The town is now much busier than depicted here, and many of its inhabitants commute to nearby Bristol.

Congresbury, The Village c1965 C234022
The place takes its name from St Congar who is said to have founded a church here. Seeking shade, he stuck his staff of yew into the ground, which then grew into a tree. The ancient market cross, on its tiered pedestal of much-worn stones, stands outside the Ship and Castle Inn.

Wrington
Broad Street c1965 W186020
Looking from its junction with Silver Street and High Street, little has changed during the last 35 years. Amors Stores, The Golden Lion, Post Office and red telephone box and petrol pumps, just beyond, are all still there. However, a bank has now replaced the shop on the left carrying an advert for 'Typhoo Tea'.

Highbridge Church Street c1950

h499003

The station at Highbridge once had seven platforms and a line ran via the level crossing, seen here, to the neighbouring resort of Burnham. There had also been an engine works employing over 300 men, but that closed in 1930. However, the Lamb Guest House and George Hotel are still there, though the latter has lost its impressive porch.

The Northern Somerset Levels

Highbridge
The River Brue 1903 50174
Barely above sea level, this expanse of dead-flat land would once have regularly been inundated by the tide and the landscape a vast salt marsh. Drainage schemes and barriers have settled the River Brue in its present course, creating agricultural land. Looking upstream from Huntsbill Road, the photograph shows Brue Farm, a view that is little changed today.

Brent Knoll
General View 1913
65395
Brent Knoll, from which the village takes its name, is the site of an Iron Age encampment, and was later quarried for lias - a local stone. Legend credits its creation to the devil who, when excavating Cheddar Gorge, flung a spadeful of earth that landed short of the sea. The buildings are the 19th-century 'Old Manor House' and St Michael's Church.

Brent Knoll, The Village and Church 1903 50177

Church Lane climbs to St Michael's, which is noted for three carved wooden bench ends showing animals dressed as an abbot and monks. They reputedly depict the victory of the parish priest over the abbot in a disagreement concerning revenues. The cottages in the photograph, originally constructed for farm workers, have since been replaced by more modern dwellings.

Brent Knoll, Battleborough 1913 65396

Battleborough is locally known as 'Arnie's House', remembering a previous occupant. Parts of the house are Tudor, and although it was altered in 1830, it retains a fascinating coat of arms on its wall. Some local stories credit its name to being the scene of a Civil War skirmish, while others claim a much older Saxon origin.

Wedmore The Borough 1950 W169021

In 878, Alfred the Great agreed a treaty here with the Danes, and Guthrum, their defeated leader, accepted Christianity. It is an attractive village, having some interesting architecture. Notice the Italianate tower, left of centre, built in 1830. Although it has been demolished, the building above which it rose survives. Once a ladies' fashion house, it now houses a chemist.

◄ **Wedmore**
The Village c1955

W169034

Built at the beginning of the 19th century, Elmsett Hall on Glanville Road was, at this time, a Hotel and Country Club, and it too was adorned with an impressive tower. Today it serves as a nursing home. Looking quite ancient, the thatched cottage opposite, Beggar's Roost, in fact dates from only 1930 and is now a private house.

Meare
The Fish House 1904
52057

Until the Dissolution, the area was part of the Glastonbury monastic estates, and the villagers made their living by fishing, selling their produce to the abbey. This church-like building, to which a roof has now been restored, was built in the 14th century and served the fisherfolk, who salted and stored their catch here.

Meare
The Village c1955
M265002
For most of its history, marshy lakes have surrounded Meare. Archaeologists have discovered villages, founded on wooden piles or brushwood rafts, from at least the 3rd century BC. This view, however, along St Mary's Road towards the war memorial, is definitely terra firma, and, although immediately recognisable today, the Ring O'Bells Inn closed some 15 years ago.

Glastonbury
The Tor 1890 23918
Rising abruptly out of the Somerset Levels, the Tor appears much higher than its 518 feet determined by survey. Instantly recognisable from afar by the isolated tower on its summit, all that remains of 14th-century St Michael's Church, it must have served as a welcome guide to the medieval pilgrims who flocked to Glastonbury.

Glastonbury
General View 1927
80558
Looking from nearby Wearyall Hill, many of the town's main landmarks can be identified. The 15th-century tower of St John's Church rises in the centre, while that to the left belongs to St Benedict's. The abbey ruins and the abbot's kitchen lie to the right, and across the road, to the left, is the cricket ground.

Glastonbury
The Abbey, The Holy Thorn 1912 64488

The new visitor centre, opened in 1989, replaces this view of the former ticket office and lodge keeper's cottage. Several of the biannually flowering holy thorns grow around the town, a sprig of which is presented to the Queen and her mother each Christmas. They traditionally derive from the original bush that sprang from Joseph's staff on Wearyall Hill.

Glastonbury, The George Hotel 1890 23908
The George Hotel was originally founded during the reign of Edward III to provide accommodation for pilgrims arriving in the town. It retains the intricate gothic façade resulting from its rebuilding in the 15th century. Here, the porter stands waiting outside, smartly dressed in waistcoat and bowler hat.

Glastonbury
The Cross 1927 80561
Local tales say the original market cross was a victim of drunken vandalism and this ornate Victorian Gothic replacement appeared in 1846. Today, the Crown Hotel is a backpackers' hostel offering budget accommodation at £10 per night. Very reasonable, but if the cameraman had stayed after taking his photograph, the bill, including dinner, would have been just 12 shillings.

Glastonbury High Street 1909 61541

Workmen take a break while boys wearing knickerbocker trousers pause to watch the photographer about his business outside the George Hotel. To the right, a delivery boy's bicycle stands by the kerb and the horse-drawn carts, further up the street, are parked outside the Tribunal building, built in the 15th century as a merchant's house and store.

Butleigh The Vale of Avalon c1960 B866008

Taken from below Windmill Hill near Butleigh, the view looks out across the Somerset Levels to Glastonbury Tor. Schemes to drain the fens and control the regular spates of flood preoccupied its inhabitants for centuries, and, from a vantage such as this, it is not difficult to imagine the whole area as a brackish lake.

Dundon The Church and Vicarage 1904 52524

St Andrew's Church possesses one of the oldest yew trees in the country. Recent tests have shown it to be some 1,700 years old, now hollow inside, there is standing room for four or five people. Once, every village had its assortment of tradesmen, something not often seen today, but a thatcher can still be found in Dundon.

Portishead The Pier 1887 20185
With deep water immediately offshore, Brunel conceived a plan for a trans-Atlantic port here. The pier was erected to accommodate his ship, the Great Western, and the nearby Royal Hotel built to cater for passengers. Towards the end of the 19th century, steam had not entirely replaced sail, and beyond the pier, a sailing ship lies at anchor.

Seaside Somerset

Portishead from Battery Point 1924 76003
Although an attempt was made to develop Portishead as a resort, it did not realise the success achieved elsewhere on the coast and its beach here is almost deserted. Battery Point commands a fine view across the Channel, and its defensive qualities have been exploited several times since it was first used as a fort by Iron Age people.

Clevedon Marine Parade 1913 65397
Although less popular than neighbouring Weston, Clevedon's visitors valued its refined quietness. Among its distinguished visitors were Tennyson, Thackeray, Sir John Betjeman and Coleridge, who came here on honeymoon. Horse-drawn carriages wait for fares among the people strolling along the sea front, while the more adventurous dabble between the rowing boats left beached by the last tide.

YA
5517

Clevedon
The Esplanade 1923
74008

Ten years later, the motorcar has replaced the horse and carriage, but the drivers have no difficulty in finding somewhere to park. The photographer has undoubtedly captured the interest of the promenaders, but nobody seems attracted to the beach.

Clevedon, The Pier 1892 31251
The pier was opened in 1869, and in comparison to that at neighbouring Weston, its construction is light and graceful, looking far too delicate to survive the storms that periodically wreak havoc along the coast. Here, behind the fishing boats, are some bathing machines, drawn down to the water's edge, ready for use.

Clevedon, The Pier and Pier Hotel c1965 C116048
70 years later, the pier is still standing, now with a pagoda added. Its luck ran out in 1970 when two spans collapsed, but, following restoration, is again open for business. A board on the ticket office lists the various entrance charges, and next to it is a weight machine - at one time a common sight.

Clevedon
Main Street 1925 77665

In keeping with its genteel promenade, the lower town also had an attractive centre. The W H Smith's shop is still there, although its window displays today are nothing like as attractive as this. The clock in the square, which also serves as a drinking fountain, is typically Victorian and has attractive glazed tiles set into its decoration.

THE CLEVEDON DEPOSITORY
DYERS

Clevedon
Hill Road 1913 65406
At the top of the town, impressive façades line Hill Road. Challicom's, the store on the left selling household goods, is still there; displayed outside are deckchairs, a bath chair and rolls of carpet. Horse carts and bicycles are still the main means of transport, but even so, it appears necessary to protect the base of the lamp standard.

63
61
H. SEELEY & CO
61
Pullin's
POLICE NOTICE
NO
WAITING

Clevedon
Hill Road c1955

C116042

A later photograph shows the same street from the opposite end. It is not much different from today's scene. The booksellers, H Seeley & Co, have just celebrated their centenary, No 63 continues to trade in ladies fashions and a loaf of bread can still be bought from Pullins Bakers, which was established in 1925.

Clevedon, Walton Castle, The Keep 1913 65423
Standing on top of Castle Hill, a mile north-west of the town, is this curious building, which was built as a folly in the 17th century. Viewed through a gap in the surrounding wall, the castle is shown in a ruinous state. Today, surrounded by the town's golf course, it has been restored as a private residence.

East Clevedon, The Village 1913 65415
Looking from the Triangle along Walton Road today, the Old Inn is recognisable on the right. Outside stands a woman beside a cart and two neatly dressed boys are obviously fascinated by the work of the photographer. Motorised transport was then still a rare phenomenon, but as you can see, the horses that preceded them created their own pollution problems.

Weston-super-Mare, The Grand Pier 1904 53003
The pier had only just opened that year, and a sign at its entrance advertises the fact. Admission was 2d, but a combined ticket gave entrance to the Pavilion Theatre, at its end, as well. It was a great success, and the theatre was destined to boast an impressive list of stars, including Sir Ralph Richardson.

GRAND PIER
DANCING
THE WORLD'S FINEST COVERED AMUSEMENT PARK!
OME
RAND PIER
CAFETERIAS
BUFFETS
REAM

Weston-super-Mare The Grand Pier c1955 W69079

Still a great success and hedging its bets against the unpredictability of the English weather, the pier confidently promotes itself as the 'worlds finest covered amusement park'. Look carefully, and you will see that the Pavilion has changed. The original was destroyed by fire in 1930, but its replacement, which opened three years later, was even bigger and became a funfair.

Weston-super-Mare The Esplanade 1904
53015
To the right a crane and workman are completing the construction of the pier. Horse-drawn cabs line the road, waiting for fares, while at the far end are electric trams, the service having begun just two years earlier. The Grand Atlantic Hotel, with its conical turrets, had opened in 1889 to cater for the ever-increasing number of summer visitors.

Weston-super-Mare Anchor Head Pier 1887

20336

Small sailing boats wait below the Royal Pier Hotel, to take passengers on pleasure trips. Ahead, lies Birnbeck Island and its pier, which opened in 1867 and was such a tremendous attraction that it had over 120,000 visitors in the first three months. As well as offering amusements, it also served as a landing stage for passenger steamers from South Wales.

Weston-super-Mare Madeira Cove 1913
65356
Here, the promenade sweeps below the road around Maderia Cove. 15 years later, the cove was enclosed by a causeway to create Marine Lake. Another sea front addition was the Rozel Bandstand, built in 1937. Before it was swept away during a storm in 1983, audiences would gather on the balcony above the Rozel Café to listen to the music.

Weston-super-Mare View from the Pier 1887 20330
Arrival by sea was as popular as rail, particularly for Welsh holidaymakers, and a trolley was employed to transfer luggage to the shore. At one time, as many as 750,000 people landed each year, but the last steam ship embarked in 1971 and the pier has now become unsafe. The Friends of the Old Pier are working to reopen it.

Worle The Village 1896 38460
Weston has now all but absorbed Worle, but this and the next scene in the old village remain identifiable. Children walk at the far end of the street, which at this date has not been sealed with tar. The shops occupying the row of cottages by The Scaurs, one of which belonged to W Robins, Dyer and Cleaner, have now gone.

Worle
The Village c1955 W184005
Not far from the Old King's Head, this later view looks along narrow lanes towards St Martin's Church. The church was founded in the 12th century but largely rebuilt some 250 years later. Inside are a row of beautifully carved misericord seats, reputed to have come from Woodspring Priory, and an interesting 15th-century stone pulpit.

Worle, High Street c1955 W184010
Worle was once able to support three butchers shops, although there are none there today. This picture shows Reynolds, one of those establishments, on the right. Next door a delivery wagon has stopped outside the Maltings. At that time this building housed a busy laundry, but now it has been converted into shops.

Burnham-on-Sea, The Beach 1907 58692
Before the 19th century Burnham was little more than a village and it was not until the fashion for 'sea-water cures' and seaside holidays arrived that it developed as a town. Carriages wait on the sand while their overdressed passengers take their exercise on the beach and then, as now, there are donkeys for the children.

Burnham-on-Sea, from the West 1918 68572
The view, taken shortly after the pier opened in 1911, shows holidaymakers enjoying the sun along the Esplanade. In contrast with today's scene, dress is rather formal, even on the beach. A clergyman sits in a bath chair talking to his companion, while a young child, almost hidden behind its pram, is helping mother to push.

Burnham-on-Sea, The Sands 1926 79284
Taken a few years later, holidaymakers now appear more relaxed, although few women have removed their hats. Children dig in the sand with their trouser legs rolled up, the fashion for itchy, hand-knitted swimming trunks and bathing costumes yet to appear. Bathing machines protect the modesty of those wanting to swim and, besides donkeys, there are swing-boats to provide amusement.

Burnham-on-Sea The Public Gardens 1907 58702

The Manor House and its gardens were built in 1841 for George Reed, one of Burnham's leading citizens. He later gave the gardens to the town and here, strollers and the gardener mowing the grass, pose for the camera. The signs by the neatly coppiced tree stumps warn that dogs must be kept on a lead.

Burnham-on-Sea
The Lighthouse and Ellen's Cottage 1887 20086
Burnham's first modern lighthouse, the Round Tower, was erected in 1800 on the sea front near the church. It was replaced by this building, known as the Bottle Lighthouse, in 1832. However it was found to be too low because of the Channel's extreme tides. A wooden structure, which still stands on the shore, was built to complement it.

Index

Frith Book Co Titles

www.francisfrith.co.uk

The Frith Book Company publishes over 100 new titles each year. A selection of those currently available are listed below. For latest catalogue please contact Frith Book Co.

Town Books 96 pages, approx 100 photos. County and Themed Books 128 pages, approx 150 photos (unless specified). All titles hardback laminated case and jacket except those indicated pb (paperback)

Title	ISBN	Price
Amersham, Chesham & Rickmansworth (pb)	1-85937-340-2	£9.99
Ancient Monuments & Stone Circles	1-85937-143-4	£17.99
Aylesbury (pb)	1-85937-227-9	£9.99
Bakewell	1-85937-113-2	£12.99
Barnstaple (pb)	1-85937-300-3	£9.99
Bath (pb)	1-85937-419-0	£9.99
Bedford (pb)	1-85937-205-8	£9.99
Berkshire (pb)	1-85937-191-4	£9.99
Berkshire Churches	1-85937-170-1	£17.99
Blackpool (pb)	1-85937-382-8	£9.99
Bognor Regis (pb)	1-85937-431-x	£9.99
Bournemouth	1-85937-067-5	£12.99
Bradford (pb)	1-85937-204-x	£9.99
Brighton & Hove(pb)	1-85937-192-2	£8.99
Bristol (pb)	1-85937-264-3	£9.99
British Life A Century Ago (pb)	1-85937-213-9	£9.99
Buckinghamshire (pb)	1-85937-200-7	£9.99
Camberley (pb)	1-85937-222-8	£9.99
Cambridge (pb)	1-85937-422-0	£9.99
Cambridgeshire (pb)	1-85937-420-4	£9.99
Canals & Waterways (pb)	1-85937-291-0	£9.99
Canterbury Cathedral (pb)	1-85937-179-5	£9.99
Cardiff (pb)	1-85937-093-4	£9.99
Carmarthenshire	1-85937-216-3	£14.99
Chelmsford (pb)	1-85937-310-0	£9.99
Cheltenham (pb)	1-85937-095-0	£9.99
Cheshire (pb)	1-85937-271-6	£9.99
Chester	1-85937-090-x	£12.99
Chesterfield	1-85937-378-x	£9.99
Chichester (pb)	1-85937-228-7	£9.99
Colchester (pb)	1-85937-188-4	£8.99
Cornish Coast	1-85937-163-9	£14.99
Cornwall (pb)	1-85937-229-5	£9.99
Cornwall Living Memories	1-85937-248-1	£14.99
Cotswolds (pb)	1-85937-230-9	£9.99
Cotswolds Living Memories	1-85937-255-4	£14.99
County Durham	1-85937-123-x	£14.99
Croydon Living Memories	1-85937-162-0	£9.99
Cumbria	1-85937-101-9	£14.99
Dartmoor	1-85937-145-0	£14.99
Derby (pb)	1-85937-367-4	£9.99
Derbyshire (pb)	1-85937-196-5	£9.99
Devon (pb)	1-85937-297-x	£9.99
Dorset (pb)	1-85937-269-4	£9.99
Dorset Churches	1-85937-172-8	£17.99
Dorset Coast (pb)	1-85937-299-6	£9.99
Dorset Living Memories	1-85937-210-4	£14.99
Down the Severn	1-85937-118-3	£14.99
Down the Thames (pb)	1-85937-278-3	£9.99
Down the Trent	1-85937-311-9	£14.99
Dublin (pb)	1-85937-231-7	£9.99
East Anglia (pb)	1-85937-265-1	£9.99
East London	1-85937-080-2	£14.99
East Sussex	1-85937-130-2	£14.99
Eastbourne	1-85937-061-6	£12.99
Edinburgh (pb)	1-85937-193-0	£8.99
England in the 1880s	1-85937-331-3	£17.99
English Castles (pb)	1-85937-434-4	£9.99
English Country Houses	1-85937-161-2	£17.99
Essex (pb)	1-85937-270-8	£9.99
Exeter	1-85937-126-4	£12.99
Exmoor	1-85937-132-9	£14.99
Falmouth	1-85937-066-7	£12.99
Folkestone (pb)	1-85937-124-8	£9.99
Glasgow (pb)	1-85937-190-6	£9.99
Gloucestershire	1-85937-102-7	£14.99
Great Yarmouth (pb)	1-85937-426-3	£9.99
Greater Manchester (pb)	1-85937-266-x	£9.99
Guildford (pb)	1-85937-410-7	£9.99
Hampshire (pb)	1-85937-279-1	£9.99
Hampshire Churches (pb)	1-85937-207-4	£9.99
Harrogate	1-85937-423-9	£9.99
Hastings & Bexhill (pb)	1-85937-131-0	£9.99
Heart of Lancashire (pb)	1-85937-197-3	£9.99
Helston (pb)	1-85937-214-7	£9.99
Hereford (pb)	1-85937-175-2	£9.99
Herefordshire	1-85937-174-4	£14.99
Hertfordshire (pb)	1-85937-247-3	£9.99
Horsham (pb)	1-85937-432-8	£9.99
Humberside	1-85937-215-5	£14.99
Hythe, Romney Marsh & Ashford	1-85937-256-2	£9.99

Available from your local bookshop or from the publisher

Frith Book Co Titles (continued)

Title	ISBN	Price
Ipswich (pb)	1-85937-424-7	£9.99
Ireland (pb)	1-85937-181-7	£9.99
Isle of Man (pb)	1-85937-268-6	£9.99
Isles of Scilly	1-85937-136-1	£14.99
Isle of Wight (pb)	1-85937-429-8	£9.99
Isle of Wight Living Memories	1-85937-304-6	£14.99
Kent (pb)	1-85937-189-2	£9.99
Kent Living Memories	1-85937-125-6	£14.99
Lake District (pb)	1-85937-275-9	£9.99
Lancaster, Morecambe & Heysham (pb)	1-85937-233-3	£9.99
Leeds (pb)	1-85937-202-3	£9.99
Leicester	1-85937-073-x	£12.99
Leicestershire (pb)	1-85937-185-x	£9.99
Lincolnshire (pb)	1-85937-433-6	£9.99
Liverpool & Merseyside (pb)	1-85937-234-1	£9.99
London (pb)	1-85937-183-3	£9.99
Ludlow (pb)	1-85937-176-0	£9.99
Luton (pb)	1-85937-235-x	£9.99
Maidstone	1-85937-056-x	£14.99
Manchester (pb)	1-85937-198-1	£9.99
Middlesex	1-85937-158-2	£14.99
New Forest	1-85937-128-0	£14.99
Newark (pb)	1-85937-366-6	£9.99
Newport, Wales (pb)	1-85937-258-9	£9.99
Newquay (pb)	1-85937-421-2	£9.99
Norfolk (pb)	1-85937-195-7	£9.99
Norfolk Living Memories	1-85937-217-1	£14.99
Northamptonshire	1-85937-150-7	£14.99
Northumberland Tyne & Wear (pb)	1-85937-281-3	£9.99
North Devon Coast	1-85937-146-9	£14.99
North Devon Living Memories	1-85937-261-9	£14.99
North London	1-85937-206-6	£14.99
North Wales (pb)	1-85937-298-8	£9.99
North Yorkshire (pb)	1-85937-236-8	£9.99
Norwich (pb)	1-85937-194-9	£8.99
Nottingham (pb)	1-85937-324-0	£9.99
Nottinghamshire (pb)	1-85937-187-6	£9.99
Oxford (pb)	1-85937-411-5	£9.99
Oxfordshire (pb)	1-85937-430-1	£9.99
Peak District (pb)	1-85937-280-5	£9.99
Penzance	1-85937-069-1	£12.99
Peterborough (pb)	1-85937-219-8	£9.99
Piers	1-85937-237-6	£17.99
Plymouth	1-85937-119-1	£12.99
Poole & Sandbanks (pb)	1-85937-251-1	£9.99
Preston (pb)	1-85937-212-0	£9.99
Reading (pb)	1-85937-238-4	£9.99
Romford (pb)	1-85937-319-4	£9.99
Salisbury (pb)	1-85937-239-2	£9.99
Scarborough (pb)	1-85937-379-8	£9.99
St Albans (pb)	1-85937-341-0	£9.99
St Ives (pb)	1-85937415-8	£9.99
Scotland (pb)	1-85937-182-5	£9.99
Scottish Castles (pb)	1-85937-323-2	£9.99
Sevenoaks & Tunbridge	1-85937-057-8	£12.99
Sheffield, South Yorks (pb)	1-85937-267-8	£9.99
Shrewsbury (pb)	1-85937-325-9	£9.99
Shropshire (pb)	1-85937-326-7	£9.99
Somerset	1-85937-153-1	£14.99
South Devon Coast	1-85937-107-8	£14.99
South Devon Living Memories	1-85937-168-x	£14.99
South Hams	1-85937-220-1	£14.99
Southampton (pb)	1-85937-427-1	£9.99
Southport (pb)	1-85937-425-5	£9.99
Staffordshire	1-85937-047-0	£12.99
Stratford upon Avon	1-85937-098-5	£12.99
Suffolk (pb)	1-85937-221-x	£9.99
Suffolk Coast	1-85937-259-7	£14.99
Surrey (pb)	1-85937-240-6	£9.99
Sussex (pb)	1-85937-184-1	£9.99
Swansea (pb)	1-85937-167-1	£9.99
Tees Valley & Cleveland	1-85937-211-2	£14.99
Thanet (pb)	1-85937-116-7	£9.99
Tiverton (pb)	1-85937-178-7	£9.99
Torbay	1-85937-063-2	£12.99
Truro	1-85937-147-7	£12.99
Victorian and Edwardian Cornwall	1-85937-252-x	£14.99
Victorian & Edwardian Devon	1-85937-253-8	£14.99
Victorian & Edwardian Kent	1-85937-149-3	£14.99
Vic & Ed Maritime Album	1-85937-144-2	£17.99
Victorian and Edwardian Sussex	1-85937-157-4	£14.99
Victorian & Edwardian Yorkshire	1-85937-154-x	£14.99
Victorian Seaside	1-85937-159-0	£17.99
Villages of Devon (pb)	1-85937-293-7	£9.99
Villages of Kent (pb)	1-85937-294-5	£9.99
Villages of Sussex (pb)	1-85937-295-3	£9.99
Warwickshire (pb)	1-85937-203-1	£9.99
Welsh Castles (pb)	1-85937-322-4	£9.99
West Midlands (pb)	1-85937-289-9	£9.99
West Sussex	1-85937-148-5	£14.99
West Yorkshire (pb)	1-85937-201-5	£9.99
Weymouth (pb)	1-85937-209-0	£9.99
Wiltshire (pb)	1-85937-277-5	£9.99
Wiltshire Churches (pb)	1-85937-171-x	£9.99
Wiltshire Living Memories	1-85937-245-7	£14.99
Winchester (pb)	1-85937-428-x	£9.99
Windmills & Watermills	1-85937-242-2	£17.99
Worcester (pb)	1-85937-165-5	£9.99
Worcestershire	1-85937-152-3	£14.99
York (pb)	1-85937-199-x	£9.99
Yorkshire (pb)	1-85937-186-8	£9.99
Yorkshire Living Memories	1-85937-166-3	£14.99

See Frith books on the internet www.francisfrith.co.uk

Frith Products & Services

Francis Frith would doubtless be pleased to know that the pioneering publishing venture he started in 1860 still continues today. A hundred and forty years later, The Francis Frith Collection continues in the same innovative tradition and is now one of the foremost publishers of vintage photographs in the world. Some of the current activities include:

Interior Decoration

Today Frith's photographs can be seen framed and as giant wall murals in thousands of pubs, restaurants, hotels, banks, retail stores and other public buildings throughout the country. In every case they enhance the unique local atmosphere of the places they depict and provide reminders of gentler days in an increasingly busy and frenetic world.

Product Promotions

Frith products are used by many major companies to promote the sales of their own products or to reinforce their own history and heritage. Frith promotions have been used by Hovis bread, Courage beers, Scots Porage Oats, Colman's mustard, Cadbury's foods, Mellow Birds coffee, Dunhill pipe tobacco, Guinness, and Bulmer's Cider.

Genealogy and Family History

As the interest in family history and roots grows world-wide, more and more people are turning to Frith's photographs of Great Britain for images of the towns, villages and streets where their ancestors lived; and, of course, photographs of the churches and chapels where their ancestors were christened, married and buried are an essential part of every genealogy tree and family album.

Frith Products

All Frith photographs are available Framed or just as Mounted Prints and Posters (size 23 x 16 inches). These may be ordered from the address below. From time to time other products - Address Books, Calendars, Table Mats, etc - are available.

The Internet

Already twenty thousand Frith photographs can be viewed and purchased on the internet through the Frith websites and a myriad of partner sites.

For more detailed information on Frith companies and products, look at these sites:

www.francisfrith.co.uk
www.francisfrith.com
(for North American visitors)

See the complete list of Frith Books at:
www.francisfrith.co.uk

This web site is regularly updated with the latest list of publications from the Frith Book Company. If you wish to buy books relating to another part of the country that your local bookshop does not stock, you may purchase on-line.

For further information, trade, or author enquiries please contact us at the address below:
The Francis Frith Collection, Frith's Barn, Teffont, Salisbury, Wiltshire, England SP3 5QP.
Tel: +44 (0)1722 716 376 Fax: +44 (0)1722 716 881 Email: sales@francisfrith.co.uk

See Frith books on the internet www.francisfrith.co.uk

To receive your FREE Mounted Print

Mounted Print
Overall size 14 x 11 inches

Cut out this Voucher and return it with your remittance for £1.95 to cover postage and handling, to UK addresses. For overseas addresses please include £4.00 post and handling.
Choose any photograph included in this book. Your SEPIA print will be A4 in size, and mounted in a cream mount with burgundy rule line, overall size 14 x 11 inches.

Order additional Mounted Prints at HALF PRICE (only £7.49 each*)
If there are further pictures you would like to order, possibly as gifts for friends and family, purchase them at half price (no additional postage and handling required).

Have your Mounted Prints framed*
For an additional £14.95 per print you can have your chosen Mounted Print framed in an elegant polished wood and gilt moulding, overall size 16 x 13 inches (no additional postage and handling required).

*** IMPORTANT!**
These special prices are only available if ordered using the original voucher on this page (no copies permitted) and at the same time as your free Mounted Print, for delivery to the same address

Frith Collectors' Guild

From time to time we publish a magazine of news and stories about Frith photographs and further special offers of Frith products. If you would like 12 months FREE membership, please return this form.

Send completed forms to:
The Francis Frith Collection, Frith's Barn, Teffont, Salisbury, Wiltshire SP3 5QP

Voucher for FREE and Reduced Price Frith Prints

Picture no.	Page number	Qty	Mounted @ £7.49	Framed + £14.95	Total Cost
		1	**Free of charge***	£	£
			£7.49	£	£
			£7.49	£	£
			£7.49	£	£
			£7.49	£	£
			£7.49	£	£
Please allow 28 days for delivery			*** Post & handling**		**£1.95**
Book Title			**Total Order Cost**		**£**

Please do not photocopy this voucher. Only the original is valid, so please cut it out and return it to us.

I enclose a cheque / postal order for £ ....
made payable to 'The Francis Frith Collection'
OR please debit my Mastercard / Visa / Switch / Amex card
(credit cards please on all overseas orders)

Number ....
Issue No (Switch only) .... Valid from (Amex/Switch) ....
Expires .... Signature ....

Name Mr/Mrs/Ms ....
Address ....
....
....
.... Postcode ....
Daytime Tel No .... Valid to 31/12/02

The Francis Frith Collectors' Guild

Please enrol me as a member for 12 months free of charge.

Name Mr/Mrs/Ms ....
Address ....
....
....
.... Postcode ....

Free Print - see overleaf

Would you like to find out more about Francis Frith?

We have recently recruited some entertaining speakers who are happy to visit local groups, clubs and societies to give an illustrated talk documenting Frith's travels and photographs. If you are a member of such a group and are interested in hosting a presentation, we would love to hear from you.

Our speakers bring with them a small selection of our local town and county books, together with sample prints. They are happy to take orders. A small proportion of the order value is donated to the group who have hosted the presentation. The talks are therefore an excellent way of fundraising for small groups and societies.

Can you help us with information about any of the Frith photographs in this book?

We are gradually compiling an historical record for each of the photographs in the Frith archive. It is always fascinating to find out the names of the people shown in the pictures, as well as insights into the shops, buildings and other features depicted.

If you recognize anyone in the photographs in this book, or if you have information not already included in the author's caption, do let us know. We would love to hear from you, and will try to publish it in future books or articles.

Our production team

Frith books are produced by a small dedicated team at offices in the converted Grade II listed 18th-century barn at Teffont near Salisbury, illustrated above. Most have worked with the Frith Collection for many years. All have in common one quality: they have a passion for the Frith Collection. The team is constantly expanding, but currently includes:

Jason Buck, John Buck, Douglas Burns, Heather Crisp, Isobel Hall, Rob Hames, Hazel Heaton, Peter Horne, James Kinnear, Tina Leary, Hannah Marsh, Eliza Sackett, Terence Sackett, Sandra Sanger, Shelley Tolcher, Susanna Walker, Clive Wathen and Jenny Wathen.